1 MONTH OF
FREE
READING

at
www.ForgottenBooks.com

By purchasing this book you are eligible for one month membership to ForgottenBooks.com, giving you unlimited access to our entire collection of over 1,000,000 titles via our web site and mobile apps.

To claim your free month visit:
www.forgottenbooks.com/free983415

ISBN 978-0-332-67241-0
PIBN 10983415

State of Rhode Island and Providence Plantations.

ANNUAL REPORT

OF THE

Harbor Commission

MADE TO THE

GENERAL ASSEMBLY

AT ITS

JANUARY SESSION, 1919

FOR

YEAR ENDING DECEMBER 31, 1918

PROVIDENCE
1919

REPORT.

To the Honorable, the General Assembly of the State of
Rhode Island:

The Harbor Commission respectfully submits its annual
report covering a period extending from January 1, 1918,
to December 31, 1918, and embracing not only its own activities since May First but those of its predecessors for
the first four months of the year, as per the minutes and
records turned over to this Commission.

CREATION OF COMMISSION.

The Harbor Commission was created by an Act of the
General Assembly, Chapter 1669 of the Public Laws,
passed at its January Session, 1918, and approved April
19, 1918, being:

An Act in Amendment of and in addition to Chapter 144
of the General Laws, entitled "Of the Protection of Navigation," and of Chapter 473 of the Public Laws, passed
at the January Session, A. D. 1909, entitled "An Act to
Create a Commission to Formulate and Report on a Plan
for the Permanent Improvement of Navigation in the Seekonk River," and of Chapter 568 of the Public Laws,
passed at the January Session, A. D. 1910, entitled "An
Act to Authorize the Appointment of and to Define the
Powers and Duties of a State Harbor Improvement Commission in Providence, Pawtucket and East Providence,"

and the several Acts in Amendment thereof and in Addition thereto.

ORGANIZATION.

The following is the personnel of the Commission by appointments made in pursuance of said Chapter 1669:

Harry E. Windsor of Providence, Chairman, to serve until February 1, 1924.

George M. Hull of East Providence, to serve until February 1, 1922.

William S. Rogers of Newport, to serve until February 1, 1919. (To fill vacancy caused by resignation of William J. Landers, appointed April 19, 1918.)

Frank A. Page of Providence, Secretary.

The Commission has appointed Franklin N. Blake, of Pawtucket, as Commissioner of the Pawtucket River.

STATE PIER NO. 1, PROVIDENCE.

There are now two steamship companies leasing State Pier No. 1. The Fabre Line, flying the French flag, docks on the south side of the Pier, and the Chesapeake & Curtis Bay R. R. Co., under the American flag, docks on the north side. However, the contract with both tenants allows other vessels to come to the Pier to discharge or take on cargo, so that for the time being the facilities are ample for taking care of tramp vessels whose owners may desire to use the Port of Providence as a distributing or forwarding centre.

The use of the Pier by the Fabre Line during the year has been greatly reduced on account of war conditions, there having been no arrivals or departures since April. The American agents are hopeful of an early release by the French Government of some of the vessels of this line, when service to French, Italian and Portuguese ports will be resumed.

The Chesapeake & Curtis Bay R. R. Company had planned to establish a line of steamers to Baltimore in connection with a service between Baltimore and the West Indies, and, in due course, possibly, a separate line out of Providence to the West Indies. Altho this Company has been paying rent since July 1, 1918, it has found that Government restrictions on business and shipping have made it impossible to initiate this enterprise.

The U. S. Bureau of Immigration during the year has renewed its lease with the State for quarters at the Pier, and it is anticipated that immigration from Portugal and Italy may recommence by Spring, with the usual accompaniment of commerce in mechandise. The military and naval branches of the Government have shown an active interest in the Pier during the year, but the only tangible results have been the storage of munitions.

The Italian Government and the Canadian Ministry of Munitions have also used the Pier for the storage of military supplies pending shipment to Europe.

Despite the war the collections from the Pier have been the largest of any year, amounting to over $11,000.

PAWTUCKET WHARF.

The Pawtucket wharf is now ready for use as a shipping and receiving point for coastwise freight. The steel freight shed is 75 feet by 100 feet, while the total length of the quay wall available for landing freight is 700 feet.

Altho a part of the property is temporarily occupied by Roy H. Beattie, Inc., for the manufacture and shipment of cement blocks for use in building sea walls, the rest of the wharf, including the freight shed, is available and well adapted for a regular freight business with New York. Several transportation companies have interested themselves deeply in a line between Pawtucket and New York, but the difficulty of obtaining suitable boats during war time, except at prohibitive figures, has thus far kept from fruition the splendid initiative of those Pawtucket and Blackstone Valley business men who have been strenuously active in promoting the steamboat proposition.

The income from the wharf for the year, derived from tenancy and options for leasing, amounts to $4,274.99.

HARBOR LINES.

The Harbor Commissioners approved certain changes in the harbor lines at Fields Point and in Wickford Cove, and the changes were enacted into law by the General Assembly by the passage of Chapters 1619 and 1665 respectively.

CHAPTER 1619.

AN ACT Changing and Establishing the Harbor Line on the Westerly Side of Providence River Near Fields Point as Established by Senate Resolution No. 54, Passed at the January Session of the General Assembly, A. D. 1881.

It is enacted by the General Assembly as follows:

SECTION 1. That part of the harbor line on the westerly side of Providence River near Fields Point between the points marked "c" and "P" in the description of the harbor line established by the Senate Resolution No. 54, passed April 28, 1881, is hereby changed and established as follows:

Beginning at a point marked "c" on a plan designated by the Harbor Commissioners, Jan. 26, 1881, and on file in the office of the Secretary of State, which said point is in latitude south 40019.93 longitude east 42460.18 and is the same point described in Chapter 819 of the Public Laws passed at the January Session of the General Assembly A. D. 1880 as 260 feet beyond the point marked "b" on plan designed by the Harbor Commissioners October 22, 1879; thence running from said point "c" south 42° 23′ 00″ E 1100 feet in continuation of the line passing through the points "b" and "c" hereinbefore referred to, to a point marked n′ shown on the accompanying plan No. 043282, dated March 12, 1918, being in latitude south 40832.45 longitude east 43201.68; thence south 47° 37′ west, 1605.05 feet making an angle of 90° with a line passing through points "c" and n′ hereinbefore referred to, to a point marked p′ on the said plan No. 043282, said point being in latitude south 41914.39 longitude east 42016.11; thence running south 2° 01′ 37″ west 5929.77 feet making an angle of 134° 24′ 37″ with the line n′ p′ to a point marked p′ in latitude south 47840 45 longitude east 41806.37 and in the harbor line shown on a plan designed by the Harbor Commissioners January 26, 1881, and approved April 28, 1881, and cn file in the office of the Secretary of State.

The latitudes of points are given in feet and hundredths southerly from a line at right angles to the meridian of the United States Coast Survey Station at Fort Independence, and situated forty thousand feet north of said station, and the longitudes are given in feet and hundredths easterly from a line parallel with the meridian of the United States Coast Survey Station at Fort Independence and situated forty thousand feet westerly thereof.

SEC. 2. Upon passage of this act, said accompanying plat shall be kept on file in the office of the Secretary of State.

SEC. 3. This act shall take effect upon its passage.

CHAPTER 1665.

AN ACT Changing and establishing the Harbor Line in Wickford Cove as established by an Act of the General Assembly by "An Act to Establish a Harbor Line in Wickford Harbor from Quonset Point to Rowe's Point, Near Brissell's Cove" Passed April 14, 1885.

Approved April 19, 1918.

It is enacted by the General Assembly as follows:

SECTION 1. That part of the harbor line in Wickford Cove between the points "w" and "y" in the description of the harbor line in Wickford Harbor established by an Act of the General Assembly April 14, 1885, is hereby changed and established as follows:

Beginning at the point marked "w" described in said Act, which point is in latitude south 121,231.85 feet, longitude east 23,824.10 feet; thence running south 33° 56′ 00″ west 264 feet to a point in the harbor line "xy" marked "a" on the accompanying plan. Said point "a" is in latitude south 121,450.89 feet, longitude 23,576.73 feet, and is in the line "xy" 111.03 feet from "x."

The latitides of points are given in feet and hundredths southerly from a line at right angles to the meridian of the United States Coast Survey Station at Fort Independence, and situated forty thousand feet north of said Station, and the longitudes are given in feet and hundredths easterly from a line parallel with the meridian of the United States Coast Survey Station at Fort Independence and situated forty thousand feet westerly thereof.

Sec. 2. Upon passage of this Act, said accompanying plat shall be kept on file in the office of the Secretary of State.

Sec. 3. This act shall take effect upon its passage.

Obstructions.

The Commission has had no serious case of obstruction in the tide waters to consider during the year.

Pollution of Tide Waters.

Attention has been given to every complaint made to the commission regarding waste and oil appearing in

Providence Harbor and upper Narragansett Bay, and vigorous measures have been taken to avoid repetition when responsibility has been located.

DREDGING.

The amount of material reported as deposited at the usual dumping ground off Prudence Island is 18,680 cubic yards. Of this amount 10,880 cubic yards consisted of sludge from the precipitation tanks of the City of Providence. The small total of material deposited at the usual dumping ground is due to the fact that a great deal of material has gone to private dumping grounds for filling in purposes under permits issued by the Commission.

LICENSES.

Licenses have been granted during the year for structures in public waters as follows:

No. 718. January 23. Standard Oil Company of New York. To fill area at Vanity Fair and extend sea wall.

No. 719. March 20. Providence Gas Company. To build a trestle at their plant at Sassafras Point.

No. 720. April 3. James McKinnon. To drive 20 piles in Seekonk River opposite north line of his property on Water Street, East Providence.

No. 721. May 22. H. N. Girard. To build wharf in Wickford Cove.

No. 722. May 22. Hamilton Web Company. To build wharf in Wickford Cove.

No. 723. May 22. Standard Oil Company of New York.

To fill area at Silver Spring; build a dike near north line of this property, and a dike from the shore to the rocks and to the north end of the sea wall under construction; and to extend sea wall to north end of Silver Spring property.

No. 724. July 24. Aberthaw Construction Company. To construct two launching ways at Fields Point and dredge area opposite, with the consent of the City of Providence.

No. 725. August 14. John R. White & Son, Inc. To build extension to wharf at Allens Avenue, Providence.

No. 726. September 25. Sayles Finishing Plant. To fill area in Seekonk River in East Providence, adjoining property, with ashes and other mill waste, the filled area to be effectively banked about with heavy material.

ASSENTS.

Assent has been given to applications as follows:

No. 1. January 2. Hamilton Web Company. To drive 84 piles in front of its premises at Wickford.

No. 2. January 9. Walter F. Seymour. To widen wharf to 12 feet.

No. 3. January 9. Narragansett Electric Lighting Company. To dredge slip at foot of Public Street, Providence, to depth of 20 feet at high tide.

No. 4. March 13. Rhode Island State Board of Public Roads. To erect concrete bridge over Narrow River in Narragansett on Boston Neck Road.

No. 5. March 27. Mexican Petroleum Corporation. To

construct two dolphins and connecting bridges fifty feet east of Kettle Point Pier.

No. 6.   April 3.   Anthony Coal & Cement Company. To dredge a channel 90 feet wide and a berth 75 feet wide to depth of 15 feet opposite their wharf in East Providence, and deposit dredged material at Prudence Island Dumping Grounds.

No. 7.   April 3.   Wickford Welfare Association.   To build a dam across Academy Cove at the Sea View Railroad Bridge in Wickford.

No. 8.   April 24.   J. S. Packard Dredging Company. To redredge berth at Olney & Payne wharf in Pawtucket to depth of 16 feet, and deposit the material at Prudence Island Dumping Grounds.

No. 9.   April 24.   Charles A. Stahl, Jr.   To drive two piles in Old Warwick Cove five feet from edge of channel opposite land of W. A. Burrows, with his consent.

No. 10.   May 1.   Glenlyon Dye Works.   To dredge small area in front of intake at its Phillipsdale works, and deposit the dredged material against the shore just south of said intake.

No. 11.   May 1.   Marie L. Champlin.   To build a wall from north line of Division Street to south line of King Street, East Greenwich.

No. 12.   May 1.   J. S. Packard Dredging Company. To deposit about 10,000 cubic yards of material at Prudence Island Dumping Grounds, dredged from berth of American Print works, Fall River, Massachusetts.

No. 13.   May 15.   East Providence Water Company. To build a coffer dam in Seekonk River at mouth of Ten

Mile River, during repairs to dam.

No. 14. May 15. Herreshoff Manufacturing Company. To install launching railway, of temporary character, for hydro-airplane pontoons in Bristol Harbor. Also to renew railway at Walker's Cove, Bristol Harbor.

No. 15. May 22. R. A. Harrington. To repair Rocky Point Wharf and to drive and fit piles at same place.

No. 16. May 22. Namquit Worsted Mills. To repair and extend its wharf in Bristol 15 feet westward.

No. 17. May 29. Rhode Island Marine Construction and Drydock Corporation. To dredge 100,000 cubic yards of mud, etc., from its location at Portsmouth and dump same at Prudence Island Dumping Grounds.

No. 18. May 29. Rhode Island Marine Construction and Drydock Corporation. To drive piles and build wharf 300 feet out from shore line of its property at Portsmouth, and to dredge area around same to depth of 30 feet.

No. 19. June 5. James McKinnon. To fill flats and build bulkheads at No. 94 and No. 102 South Water Street, East Providence.

No. 20. June 12. J. S. Packard Dredging Company. To dredge extension of berth on north side of Seaconnet Coal Company wharf, Allens Avenue, Providence, to depth of 23 feet mean low water, and deposit the material at Standard Oil Company property at Vanity Fair, East Providence.

No. 21. June 12. Lewis Herreshoff. To rebuild his wharf at Homestead, Prudence Island.

No. 22. June 19. Staples Coal Company. To substitute new plans for building wharf in Warren for which License No. 717 was granted July 18, 1917.

No. 23. June 26. Renaldo C. Castiglioni. To build wharf at Oakland Beach.

No. 24. July 3. J. S. Packard Dredging Company. To redredge berth at City Coal Company, Pawtucket.

No. 25. July 3. J. S. Packard Dredging Company. To redredge berth at Cottrell Lumber Company, Pawtucket.

No. 26. July 3. City of Providence. To allow material dislodged by hydraulicing process of excavating hills at Fields Point to flow into Providence River inshore of the harbor line, provided that a dike of heavy material shall first be built along the shore between high and low water so that the westerly end shall be about 1,200 feet westerly of the south end of the sea wall and the easterly end shall begin at high tide near the easterly end of the fill to be made, the top of the dike not to be lower than mean high water.

No. 27. July 10. J. S. Packard Dredging Company. To dredge a channel 1,000 feet by 40 feet to a depth of 6 feet at mean low water at Sassafras Point, to furnish water for condenser intake of Providence Sewage Pumping Station; also to dump the mud (about 10,000 cubic yards) in the edge of the harbor channel, redredge the mud into larger scows and deposit same at Standard Oil Company property at Vanity Fair.

No. 28. July 10. Oakland Beach Civic League. To place seven channel markers at Brushneck Cove, Oakland Beach, with the consent of riparian owners.

No. 29. July 31. Edward V. Brown. To place fish

trap at Rumstick Point opposite Mary E. Dyer property just south of its northerly line.

No. 30. July 31. Blackstone Valley Gas and Electric Company. To dredge berth at foot of Tidewater Street, Pawtucket, to depth of 22 feet mean high water a distance of 300 feet beginning at south end of dock; also to provide new bulkhead along the dock front involved.

No. 31. August 7. Roy H. Beattie, Inc. To construct temporary pile wharf 20 feet by approximately 100 feet on west bank of Pawtucket River, with consent of S. T. Carpenter, riparian owner; also to store concrete blocks in shallow water just south, with consent of Frank A. Sayles, riparian owner, outside channel lines, for a period of not over two months.

No. 32. August 21. Standard Oil Company of New York. To repair wharf at Red Bridge, East Providence.

No. 33. August 28. Tusketucket Boat Club. To locate float at right angles from Cove Avenue in Brushneck Cove, Oakland Beach, to be extended into the water 40 feet from high water mark and to measure 10 feet by 10 feet.

No. 34. September 4. W. V. Polleys & Company. To replace piling and renew dolphins at Narragansett Boat Club on Seekonk River.

No. 35. September 11. Herreshoff Manufacturing Company, Inc. To repair piers at its main works and at Walker's Cove, Bristol, by driving replacement piles.

No. 36. September 25. Frank Paull. To drive about 25 piles at head of his wharf, 267 Thames Street, Bristol, to replace old ones.

No. 37. September 25. Newell Coal & Lumber Company. To repair its wharf at Pawtucket by strengthening present wall with a reenforced concrete mat for length of about 50 feet.

No. 38. September 25. Providence Drydock & Marine Railway Company. To drive about 20 fender spiles and relocate a portion of fender spiling at its northern pier.

No. 39. September 25. J. S. Packard Dredging Company. To dredge berth at dock of Providence Drydock & Marine Railway Company, East Providence, to depth of 25 feet mean low water, and to deposit the material at Prudence Island Dumping Grounds or at Standard Oil Company property at Vanity Fair.

No. 40. October 9. William E. Bowen. To repair Payne & Butler Oyster Wharf on east side of Seekonk River, about 800 feet south of old railroad bridge in East Providence.

No. 41. October 9. John R. White & Son, Inc. To drive and fasten 75 piles to wharf on Allens Avenue opposite Blackstone Street, Providence.

No. 42. October 18. F. C. Stender. To repair wharf of Colonial Navigation Company on South Water Street, Providence.

No. 43. December 18. Marine Engineering & Dry Dock Company. To dredge two wet slips and a location for a 3,200 ton marine railway at their leased plot on Allens Avenue, Providence.

FINANCIAL STATEMENT.

Bond Issue

Total Harbor Improvement Bond Issue....		$1,000,000 00

Total expended for land, construction and improvements:

To December 31, 1917	$922,243 27	
In Year 1918	55,742 96	$977 986 23

Unexpended Balance on Hand December 31, 1918		22,013 77
		$1,000,000 00

Care and Maintenance Account.

Appropriations:

State Harbor Improvement Commission	$7,000 00	
Expended by said Commission prior to May 1	2,190 98	

Balance available to new Harbor Commission .		$4,809 02
Seekonk River Commission	$1,387 24	
Expended by said Commission prior to May 1......	150 00	

Balance available to new
    Harbor Commission.   .   1,237 24

Total available to New Harbor Commission . $6,046 26
Expended, May 1 to December 31 . . . .   5,604 89

    Unexpended Balance December 31, 1918 $441 37

Receipts in 1918.

State Pier No. 1, Providence $11,357 75
Pawtucket Wharf 4,274 99

    Total $15,632 74

Work of the United States Engineer Department.

By courtesy of the District Engineer, U. S. A., Newport, R. I., in charge of river and harbor improvements in this district, we have been furnished with data relating to Rhode Island waters, which may be found in the appendix.

    Respectfully submitted,

        HARRY E. WINDSOR,
        GEORGE M. HULL,
        W. S. ROGERS.
            Harbor Commissioners.

APPENDIX A.

STATEMENT OF PROGRESS OF RIVER AND HARBOR IMPROVEMENTS IN THE STATE OF RHODE ISLAND JANUARY 1—DECEMBER 31, 1918.

WAR DEPARTMENT
UNITED STATES ENGINEER OFFICE
284 THAMES STREET
NEWPORT, R. I.

January 29, 1919.

Rhode Island State Harbor Commission,
Room 320, State House,
Providence, R. I.

Gentlemen:

1. Your letter of the 24th relative to commercial statistics and annual report has been received and noted.

2. I have requested the pamphlet copies of the annual report for this district for the fiscal year ending June 30, 1918, but as same has not been received, I will say that the following statement covers activities of this department in Rhode Island waters this year: January 1—December 31, 1918:

Owing to war conditions, the work of improvement of rivers and harbors was suspended except in cases of urgent necessity. Under this policy, only a small amount of work was done in Providence Harbor, resulting in securing a berth with a draft of about 23 feet at the wharf of the Providence Gas Company. Practically all of the effective dredging plant in this vicinity was commandeered for other localities regarded as of greater war urgency.

Very respectfully,

J. H. WILLARD,

Colonel U. S. Army, Retired.

APPENDIX B.

Extract from Report of the Chief of Engineers, U. S. A. for 1918.

Providence River and Harbor.

Existing project.—This provides for dredging to a depth of 30 feet at mean low water all of the harbor, about 1.6 miles in length by from 1,300 to 1,800 feet in width, from Fox Point to Fields Point, limited on the east and west sides of the harbor lines, excepting the area formerly known as Green Jacket Shoal, and for dredging to the same depth an approach channel 600 feet wide southward from Fields Point to the deep water of Narragansett Bay at a point nearly opposite North Point on Popasquash Neck. The total length of both the river and harbor included within this project is 10.4 miles. The mean tidal range is about 4.7 feet increased to 5.7 feet at time of spring tides; the tidal planes are subject to irregular fluctuations, due to storms, amounting to 2 feet. The estimate of cost for new work revised in 1915, is $1,112,600, exclusive of amounts expended under previous projects. The latest (1918) approved estimate for annual cost of maintenance is $25,000.

The existing project was authorized by the river and harbor act of March 4, 1913 (H Doc. No. 1369, 62d Cong., 3d sess.). The latest published map is in the Annual Report for 1915, page 2068.

Operations and results during fiscal year.—Work under the existing contract for dredging the 30-foot channel to Providence, in progress at the beginning of the fiscal year, was continued through December, when the unusual severity of the weather stopped all dredging. Dredging was resumed in March, 1918, and a small amount was done during that month to connect with private dredging operations carried on by the largest coal-handling plant in the harbor. The dredging was done by plant of inferior capacity, as the larger plant which had been intended for use under the contract has been commandeered for war work of greater urgency. The area increased to 30 feet depth is slight and not continuous as the effort had been to add as far as possible to the facilities of the fuel-handling plants, and to secure the full depth along the city wall where certain items of war manufacturing are being actively prosecuted. The expenditures were $29,012 98 for new work.

Condition at end of fiscal year.—The existing project is about 70 per cent completed. There is an approach channel 600 feet in width from its southern extremity, opposite the North Point on Popasquash Neck to Fields Point, a distance of about 9 miles, which has been dredged to 30 feet depth at mean low water, the limiting lines of the 30-foot deep channel in the upper part being the same as those of the 25-foot deep channel previously dredged between Gaspee Point and Fields Point. Above Fields Point the entire harbor up to Fox Point has been dredged to a depth of 25 feet and about 32 per cent of this area has been deepened to 30 feet. That portion of the harbor formerly occupied by the Green Jacket Shoal and not included in the existing project has a depth of from 21 to 26 feet of water. The total expenditure under the existing project was $767,457.92 for new work and $49,463.50 for maintenance, a total of $816,921.42.

Local cooperation.—The river and harbor act of June 25, 1910, provided that; "No part of this amount ($459,000, estimated cost of the work then provided for) shall be expended until satisfactory assurances that the city of Providence or other local agency will expend on the improvement of the harbor front in accordance with said document (H. Doc. No. 606, 61st Cong., 2d sess.) above referred to, a sum equal to the amount herein appropriated and authorized." The proper assurances were promptly given, and approved by the Secretary of War September 6, 1910.

The river and harbor act of March 4, 1913, provided as follows:

"That no work in the harbor proper north of Fields Point shall be done until the Secretary of War is satisfied that the State and city have completed their proposed expenditures in the combined Providence and Pawtucket Harbors up to at least $2,000,000 for public terminals or other permanent public harbor improvements."

This was modified by the river and harbor act of March 4, 1915 (Rivers and Harbors Committee Doc. No. 9, 63d Cong., 2d sess.), by the addition of the words—

"or shall have given to the Secretary of War assurance satisfactory to him that the expenditure of the $2,000,000 aforesaid will be completed within a time satisfactory to him and not later than three years from the passage of this amendment.''

This assurance was given the Secretary of War and was approved by him June 11, 1915. The entire amount was expended by the State of Rhode Island and city of Providence prior to March 4, 1918.

Terminal facilities.—These consist of piers and wharves with a total docking space of 29,250 feet, of which 4,800 feet is publicly owned, about 3,150 feet is open for general public use upon payment of wharfage, and 21,300 feet is privately owned and used. All of these wharves and piers are or can easily be connected with railroad lines which are in operation on all sides of the harbor. The facilities are considered adequate for existing commerce.

Effect of Improvement.—The deepening of the harbor has modified to a considerable extent the character of the vessels using it. Large steam colliers are replacing some of the coal barges formerly bringing coal from southern ports, where the trip involved a considerable ocean voyage; four large oil-producing companies have provided themselves with terminal facilities and have taken advantage of the favorable situation of Providence for southern traffic by making it a distributing center for southeastern New England, bringing their products from the Gulf of Mexico and other points in tank steamers and barges drawing from 21 to 26 feet of water. Additional land adjacent to the new channel about 1 1-4 miles south of Kettle Point is now in course of development as one of the most extensive oil-distributing plants on the North Atlantic coast. An extensive development of industrial plants is in progress at and near Fields Point.

Proposed operations.—The recent development of war industries in Providence immediately on the harbor front has been such as to render urgent the completion of the 30-foot depth in that portion of the harbor extending along the western harbor line for a width of about 400 feet as far north as the State pier, and the completion of the 30-foot depth on the east side of the harbor as far north as the wharf of the Gulf Refining Co. These industries include the fitting out and completion of vessels built under the Shipping Board, a large boiler plant operating on naval requirements, and the manufacture of coke and the toluol products in addition to large industries away from the direct water front.

It is proposed to apply the available balance or as much thereof as may be necessary to completing the 30-foot depth by dredging at the above localities, the work to be done as soon as it is possible to secure the necessary plant. No estimate for additional funds is submitted as those available are believed to be sufficient to complete the work proposed, but not the project.

PAWTUCKET (SEEKONK) RIVER.

Operations and results during the fiscal year.—No works of improvement or maintenance were in progress during the fiscal year. The expenditures were $30.33 for contingencies in connection with the supervision of private and State improvements and are charged to maintenance.

Condition at end of fiscal year.—The project was completed during the fiscal year 1913. The channel between Providence and Phillipsdale had a usable depth of 16 feet, between Phillipsdale and Pawtucket 15 feet, and between the wharves at Pawtucket from 15 to 18 feet at mean low tide. The head of navigation is at Pawtucket Falls, about 5.2 miles above the mouth of the river. The expenditure under the existing project has been $164,573.40 for new work and $7,565.69 for maintenance, a total of $172,139.09. In addition there was expended $67,792 for new work from contributed funds, a grand total of both United States and contributed funds of $239,931.09.

Local cooperation.—The river and harbor act of March 2, 1907, required that the State of Rhode Island or other agency should contribute $67,792, which was complied with.

Terminal facilities.—Including the wharves at Phillipsdale, two in number, these cover about 4,540 feet of docking space, in which 700 feet is owned by the State of Rhode Island and 3,840 feet owned and used by private owners. Of the latter some portions are at times used by the public upon payment of wharfage. The two wharves at Phillipsdale have near-by rail connections in the yards of the owners. The other wharves are not conveniently located for rail connection. The facilities are considered adequate for the exising commerce.